MAP
Illustrating History of
THE CHURCH
During the Celtic Period.
Scale of Miles

THE CHURCH
OF SCOTLAND

THE CHURCH OF SCOTLAND

*The Church of Scotland
is part of the
Universal Catholic Church …*

The Church of Scotland traces its history back to the coming of Christianity to the British Isles with the spread of the Roman Empire.

The precise extent of a Christian presence in the first centuries AD is unknown. The earliest known centres of Christian activity were at Whithorn in the south-west of Scotland at the turn of the fourth century, and on the island of Iona, off the west coast, in the sixth century. From these centres the Gospel was carried to other parts of the land under the influence of Ninian and Columba respectively.

Originally Celtic in character because of the earlier links of Ninian and Columba with France and Ireland, the Church in Scotland was gradually made to conform to the pattern which the Church had adopted on the Continent under the influence of Rome.

No one did more to bring this about than Queen Margaret of Scotland in the eleventh century because of her upbringing in England and Hungary, and for the next five centuries the Church in Scotland was indistinguishable from the rest of medieval Catholic Christendom.

*The Church of Scotland
is Protestant and Reformed ...*

The Reformation came to Scotland comparatively late. Its first martyr was burned at the stake in 1528, eleven years after Martin Luther launched his attack on the Church with his 95 theses. But, as in other countries of Europe, it was brought about by the same combination of factors – spiritual, political, social, economic and intellectual – and by the excessive power and corruption of the clergy.

In Scotland the movement for reform found its popular leader in John Knox, although much of his early life was spent outside the country. By the time he returned in 1559, Knox had gained a wide experience of Protestantism as a minister in Switzerland, France, Germany and England.

In 1560 the Scottish Parliament officially adopted Protestantism as the nation's religion, outlawed the Mass, and approved a Confession of Faith and the reorganisation of the Church along Protestant lines.

The country was divided into parishes. In each parish a Kirk Session was formed consisting of the minister and a number of elders, and once a year the Church would meet in General Assembly to oversee all its work.

Many characteristic features associated with the Church of Scotland over the years – its emphasis on the Bible and preaching, simplicity in worship, and on the priesthood of all believers – stem from John Knox and the Reformation he led.

3

4

*The Church of Scotland
is Presbyterian ...*

The full flowering of the
Reformation in terms of church
polity emerged some twenty to
thirty years later through the
influence of Andrew Melville. His
Second Book of Discipline (1581) laid
down the complete Presbyterian
system of church courts – Kirk
Session, Presbytery, Synod, and
General Assembly.

This arrangement was accepted by
Parliament in 1592. However, it took
a further hundred years of often
bitter strife, in the main, against the
counter-claims of Episcopalianism,
before Presbyterianism prevailed as
'the only government of Christ's
Church within this kingdom'.

As a Presbyterian Church, the
Church of Scotland gives a
substantial place to its eldership
('lay' people ordained to serve) in
the running of its affairs. In the
Assembly and in Presbytery, elders
and ministers serve in virtually

5

equal numbers with the balance slightly in favour of the elders, while the Kirk Session is comprised of elders with the minister.

All ministers are equal in status, irrespective of years of service or of the appointment they may hold. The Moderator (the person presiding when any court meets) – even the Moderator of the General Assembly – is *primus inter pares* only (first among equals).

Women became eligible for the eldership in 1966 and for the ministry in 1968. Members of the Diaconate (which is open to men and women) were admitted to full membership of the courts of the Church in 1990. In 1980 an Auxiliary Ministry (part-time and non-stipendiary) was sanctioned.

Synods were dissolved in 1992 as they were no longer serving any useful purpose. Congregations continue to have the right to choose their minister.

The Church of Scotland is the National Church of Scotland ...

Since 1690, when Parliament restored Scottish Presbyterianism, the Church of Scotland has been the official Church of the Scottish people. The Church of Scotland's status as the national church in Scotland was further guaranteed in the Act of Union of Scotland and England of 1707.

Evidence of this privileged position is to be seen, for example:
- in the promise taken by the Sovereign in the Oath of Accession *'inviolably to maintain and preserve the Protestant Religion and Presbyterian Church Government'*;
- in the right of the Sovereign to attend the General Assembly, though not to take any part in its deliberations;
- in the place given to the Moderator of the General Assembly in terms of precedence – in Scotland next after

the Lord Chancellor of Great Britain, and in England after the Bishops of the Church of England and before the Barons;

- in the place given to the Church of Scotland to be represented officially on State occasions and on public bodies;
- and, above all, by its own acceptance of the *'distinctive call and duty to bring the ordinances of religion to the people in every parish of Scotland through a territorial ministry'*.

The Church of Scotland is a Free Church ...

Unlike many other national churches, the Church of Scotland is not State-controlled. The Sovereign is not the head of the Church as is the case in the Church of England. Parliament is not involved in any clerical appointments.

State interference in matters of doctrine, worship, government and discipline is specifically debarred.

The Church is free to set her own standards in these matters, and is the sole judge when it comes to assessing how these standards are being kept.

The relationship between Church and State is one of partnership, in the recognition that each has its own sphere of activity while 'owing mutual duties to each other' in 'promoting each other's welfare'.

The General Assembly is the supreme court of the Church and composed of a third of the active ministers of the Church and an equal number of elders, together with a commensurate number of members of the Diaconate, appointed by the presbyteries.

Presiding over it is a Moderator nominated by a special committee but elected by the Assembly, who holds office for twelve months. During that time he/she visits presbyteries and partner churches overseas and carries out various duties, representing the Church.

Belief and Worship

The Church of Scotland is some-times accused of being uncertain in matters of **doctrine**. She does allow her ministers and members a general liberty of opinion, but no such freedom is allowed in regard to points of doctrine that are of the substance of the Faith, or where the Assembly have enacted legislation.

The first of the Articles Declaratory of the Constitution of the Church of Scotland in Matters Spiritual − *'adherence to which, as interpreted by the church, is essential to its continuity and corporate life'* (Article VIII) − declares the Church of Scotland to be both Catholic and Reformed, *'Trinitarian in its creed, and evangel-ical in its character'* and holding the Word of God as contained in the Bible as its supreme rule of faith and life.

The Church of Scotland uses the ancient Creeds in its worship (some congregations more than others), but the Church of Scotland is also a Confessional Church, the Westminster Confession of Faith of 1647 being its subordinate standard.

For many the Westminster Con-fession reflects too much the spirit of its age. Attempts have been made to frame a modern Confession, but so far without success. The Church, however, has dissociated herself from those statements in the Westminster Confession that are hostile to the Roman Catholic Church and to the Pope.

The Church of Scotland is doctrinally a broad church. A large majority of its ministers and mem-bers could be termed liberal, while a growing number are noticeably theologically conservative. All will hold by the inspiration of the Bible, but many of those who are conservatively minded see the Bible as literally inspired, and for some it is totally free of error. Again, all will believe in Jesus' Incarnation and Resurrection, but not all do so in precisely the same way.

9

At its best, **worship** in the Church of Scotland is simple, dignified, and reverent. The conduct of public worship is the responsibility of the local minister, and so varies from church to church. Services will reflect the minister's personal ideas and tastes, although more and more ministers are involving members of their congregations both in planning worship and in carrying it out. Nonetheless there is a distinctive pattern.

Church of Scotland worship, by comparison with other churches, may seem to be less, or even non-liturgical. There is no Prayer Book for use by a congregation, and the book of *Common Order* which contains a variety of Orders of Service, although authorised by the General Assembly, is a guide only for ministers and others who lead public worship.

But there is a structure and a

progression in the separate elements of praise, prayer and preaching. The Word of God in Scripture is given a central place and there is opportunity for the people to make their offerings in acknowledgement of the generosity of God.

Most Services are still conducted entirely by the minister, but in some congregations members read the scripture lessons and share in responses to the prayers.

Music plays a large part in any Service. In most congregations there will be a voluntary choir led by an amateur organist, but in some of the larger congregations the organist will be a professional musician and the choir will be paid. Modern hymns, guitars and other forms of instrumental accompaniment are in use in many churches.

There has always been a strong emphasis on preaching in the Church of Scotland. Nowadays sermons tend to be shorter and many ministers spend much less time in sermon preparation than once was the case.

Only in a few congregations is the Sacrament of the Lord's Supper (Holy Communion) celebrated every Sunday. In many congregations it is celebrated only twice or four times a year. More frequent celebration however is on the increase.

At Communion Services an invitation is extended to all in membership of the Church to join in taking the bread and wine, for in the Church of Scotland the Table is seen to be the Lord's Table and not the Church's. The elements of bread and wine are usually taken to the people, but sometimes the people are invited to gather round the Table, where they will pass the elements from person to person. The bread may be prepared in advance in small diced portions for individual use, or it may come in small slices or loaves from which each communicant takes a portion

11

before passing it on. The wine, fermented or unfermented, will come either in individual glasses or in larger cups (the common cup) which is passed around and from which people drink in turn.

Few congregations hold Sunday evening services, but some hold two morning services. Particularly in rural districts, where several congregations may be linked under one minister, some may not have a service every Sunday. Midweek services are held in few churches, and almost certainly only in towns or cities.

The Church of Scotland does not make much of the Festivals of the Christian Year. Christmas Eve services have become very popular, but Services on Christmas Day and even on Easter Day are poorly attended by comparison. Holy Week Services are few in number and are even less well attended.

However, growing ecumenical links with other denominations are leading to sharing of services and the setting up of study groups, particularly during Lent.

There is wide recognition of the need for the renewal of worship, for it is an expression of the Church's faith in God and of her commitment to the Christian life. A living Church and lively worship go together.

Social and Moral Concerns

Where the Church has approved specific legislation, this can be said to express the mind of the Church. Otherwise, even statements made by a General Assembly are no more than expressions of what is felt should be generally accepted throughout the Church. This applies to a wide range of social and moral issues.

Keeping this in mind, it can be said that the Church of Scotland:

- practises both infant and adult baptism, but refuses to countenance second baptism;
- believes in marriage rather than cohabitation for heterosexual couples;
- permits ministers to remarry divorced persons;
- approves of sexual intercourse only within heterosexual marriage;
- sympathises with those who may be homosexual, but disapproves of homosexual intercourse;
- has no official Service for the blessing of homosexual relationships;
- is opposed to gambling in society generally and particularly in the raising of Church funds;
- abhors the practice of Euthanasia, and opposes action to legalise it;
- would discipline a minister, office-bearer or member found guilty of moral fault;
- rejects artificial insemination by anonymous donor (AID), egg donation, embryo donation and

13

surrogacy, but not artificial insemination by husband (AIH) or in vitro fertilisation (IVF) as treatments for infertility;

- is of the view that abortion should take place only where continued pregnancy would involve serious risk to the life, or grave injury to the health, physical or mental, of the mother, and that the legal time-limit should be reduced;

- welcomes the development of human transplant therapy and the use of animal organs and foetal material under strict safeguards;

- advocates temperance in the use of alcohol while recognising the case for total abstinence.

Administration and Special Interests

Congregations are helped in the day-to-day work in their parishes, and in the wider work of the Church, by Boards and Committees of the **General Assembly**.

All report to the **Assembly** and seek approval for future policy.

Membership is drawn from ministers, elders, members of the Diaconate, and, in some cases, members of the Church not holding any office or appointment.

Most Boards and Committees have their administrative offices at 121 George Street, Edinburgh, but the **Board of Social Responsibility** is based at Charis House, Milton Road East, and **Parish Education** at St Colm's College and Education Centre, both in Edinburgh.

* * *

The **Board of Practice and Procedure** is responsible for advising on church law and church/state relationships, for servicing meetings of the **General Assembly**, and attending to the general interests of the Church not covered by other Committees.

* * *

The **General Trustees** are the
Church's property corporation.
As well as administering properties,
they give grants and loans to
congregations for building work,
and are the central body involved
in property maintenance.

*   *   *

The **Board of Stewardship and
Finance** promotes teaching and
understanding of Christian
Stewardship, provides programmes
and training to assist congregations
in visiting members, prepares and
allocates the Church's co-ordinated
budget and provides administrative
and accounting services for the
Assembly, its Boards and Committees. Through the Mission and
Aid Fund the wider work of the
Church is financed and the money
is allocated to congregations.

*   *   *

The **Personnel Committee**
determines salaries and all other
terms and conditions of employment for members of Staff for
whom it is the employing agency –

15

whether working in the central offices or elsewhere. It is also involved in recruiting and inter-viewing new or replacement staff, as well as advising other employing agencies (except the **Board of Social Responsibility**) on certain personnel matters (*eg* contracts of employment and discipline).

* * *

The **Woman's Guild**, Scotland's largest voluntary organisation for women, co-ordinates and resources the activities of its congregational groups. In 1997, if the General Assembly so approves, it will become a new movement, taking the best of the past 110 years and adapting itself to meet the needs of contem-porary women.

For 1997-2000 its **strategic programming plan** focusses on *Riches and Poverty*. Within that, **annual themes** and **associated projects** highlight concerns, raise awareness and promote particular aspects of the Church's work at home and overseas.

Currently, the Guild's **Aim** is to unite the women of the Church in the dedication of their lives to the Lord Jesus Christ through worship, fellowship and service. It produces literature, arranges training and offers women opportunities to develop gifts, skills and confidence, and bring a Christian perspective to the issues of the day.

* * *

In consultation with Presbyteries, Boards and Committees, the **Assembly Council** assesses the changing needs, challenges and responsibilities of the Church, encourages inter-departmental dialogue and greater co-ordination in the policies of the Boards and Committees, and makes recommen-dations to the General Assembly concerning priority areas and tasks.

* * *

The **Church and Nation Committee** is required to watch over developments in the nation's life in which moral and spiritual considerations specially arise, and to

consider what action the Church from time to time may be advised to take, to further the highest interests of the people.

* * *

The **Office for Worship, Doctrine and Artistic Matters** co-ordinates the work of three committees.

The **Panel on Worship** publishes services and songs to help local churches towards worship which is fresh and dignified, and in which all feel they can take part fully.

The **Panel on Doctrine** assists the church in Assembly and in local parishes in thinking through difficult aspects of Christian belief and Christian life.

The **Advisory Committee on Artistic Matters** gives advice and help to local churches when they wish to make changes that will help enrich their life together, or beautify their churches to enrich their worship.

17

With its several special committees overseeing the wide variety of work, the **Board of National Mission** plans and resources the mission and evangelisation projects of the Church. It advises presbyteries on forward planning, maintains churches in extension charges, develops ideas and offers resources to congregations through its advisers and training centres.

It relates to chaplaincies in hospitals, prisons, industry and universities. Field staff are recruited and trained to support congregations.

The Board has links with the **Consultative Committee on Church Properties**, the **Joint Prison Chaplaincies Board** (with the Roman Catholic and Scottish Episcopal Churches) and the **Iona Community Board**.

After-school care and a Renewal Foundation for work in areas of greatest need in Scotland are among the initiatives taken by the Board.

The **Board of Ministry** is responsible for all matters relating to parish ministry, for determining the level of the minimum stipend, for pension provision for ministers, for the provision of retirement housing, supervising ministers after licensing, and for the **Diaconate Committee**.

* * *

With more than eighty care establishments and projects the **Board of Social Responsibility** is Scotland's largest social work agency in the voluntary sector. Over forty homes care for around 1050 elderly people.

Other work includes counselling and support centres, residential units for those with drug and alcohol dependency, those in need of specialised care, and projects for homeless people.

The Board offers guidance to the Church on social, moral and ethical issues: subjects examined by

study groups have included child abuse, gambling, euthanasia, and human genetics.

Service users, the government and local authorities provide most of the Board's finance and the Church's Mission and Aid Fund also contributes towards costs.

* * *

The **Board of World Mission** aims to enable the membership of the Church of Scotland to experience and enjoy being part of the world-wide Church, sharing in its mission, as partners with other churches in the work of seeking God's Kingdom on earth.

It works in partnership with churches in over thirty countries and appoints ministers to churches in Europe and Israel.

The work of the Board involves many aspects of mission including education, healing, community development and evangelism. It has direct links with **Christian Aid**.

19

* * *

The Church of Scotland is fully committed to the modern ecumenical movement, and has given the **Committee on Ecumenical Affairs** the responsibility for encouraging all departments of the Church to increase the amount of work done with other churches.

The Committee seeks to encourage and enable the Church of Scotland to play the fullest part in the ecumenical bodies of which it is a member, including the **World Alliance of Reformed Churches**, the **World Council of Churches**, the **Conference of European Churches**, the **Council of Churches for Britain and Ireland** and **Action of Churches Together in Scotland**.

The Church is in conversation with the Roman Catholic Church in Scotland and the Scottish Episcopal Church. It also has an agreement on the recognition of ministry with the Baptist Union of Scotland.

* * *

The **Committee on Education** is the oldest continuing committee of the Church and is concerned with all aspects of educational provision in Scotland, taking special interest in religious education and school chaplaincy. It has links with the Roman Catholic Education Commission, the Scottish Joint Committee on Religious Education and Forum on Scottish Education, with whom, from time to time, it makes proposals to the Government on educational policy and principles.

The **Committee on Education for the Ministry** is responsible for recruiting and selecting candidates for the full time and auxiliary ministry, and supervising their training.

The **Board of Parish Education** is responsible for the provision of Christian education for Church members of all ages – for youth and young adult services, the training of lay agents (including Readers), curriculum development and publication (including Sunday School material), extension education, and leadership training. The Board shares with the **Committee on Education** a common concern for special educational needs.

* * *

The **Board of Communication** keeps before the Church the need for effective communication in the Church and in the world. It is responsible for **Life & Work**, the Church's monthly magazine; **Saint Andrew Press**, publishing arm of the Church; **Publicity & Design Services**, an in-house design and exhibition facility; **Pathway Productions**, the Church's audio-visual and television production unit; and the **Press Office**, which provides an information service to the Media.

* * *

There are also other Committees in the Church, like the **Committee on Chaplains to Her Majesty's Forces** whose names give a clear indication of their particular sphere of interest and responsibility.

21

ACKNOWLEDGEMENTS

The following contributors and sources are acknowledged with gratitude:

Original text written by Revd A. Gordon McGillivray, and edited by Ann Davies, Senior Press Officer of the Church of Scotland. Cover design and internal layout by Peter Forrest, Publicity & Design Department, Board of Communication. Thanks are also due to all those in the Departments and Boards of the Church of Scotland who checked and approved the appropriate sections of the manuscript and contributed photographs and illustrations.

Page (i) Map from R. H. Story (ed): *The Church of Scotland: Past and Present* (London: Wm. Mackenzie, 1890); *pages* (i),1 Stained-glass window, Chapel at 121 George Street, Edinburgh; *pages* (ii),7 Lochaline High Cross, © Paul Turner; *page* 2 John Knox portrait and signature, J. Grant: *Old and New Edinburgh* (Cassell, 1887); *page* 3 John Knox House, High Street, Edinburgh, Grant: *Old and New Edinburgh*; *pages* 4–5 'Signing the National Covenant in Greyfriars Kirkyard in 1638', J.A.Wylie: *The Scots Worthies* (London: Wm. Mackenzie, 1880); *page* 8 General Assembly of the Church of Scotland (full and detail), © Photo Express; *pages* 8–9 (and cover) Church of Scotland emblem; *page* 10 Interior of St Giles Cathedral, High Street, Edinburgh, Grant: *Old and New Edinburgh*; *pages* 12–13 'The Last Supper' and 'The Crucifixion', E. Miller: *Scripture History* (London: T. Kelly, 1840); *pages* 12–13 A Communion Table, © Roland Portchmouth; *page* 15 (top photo) Church of Scotland Offices, 121 George Street; (middle) Charis House, © Board of Social Responsibility; (bottom) Part of St Colm's College, © Chris Christenson, for Board of Parish Education; *pages* 16–17 Woman's Guild logo; *page* 17 (top) Iona Abbey, © Anne Maxwell, for the Church of Scotland; (middle) Window at Currie Session House, © Paul Turner; (bottom) Church organ; *pages* 18–19 Netherbow Theatre/ John Knox House Museum logo; *page* 19 (top) Industrial Chaplain, © Press Office, Church of Scotland; (middle) © Chris Christenson, for Board of Parish Education; (bottom) © Board of World Mission; *pages* 20–21 Ecumenical symbol; *page* 20 (top) © Kain Rutherford; (middle) Publicity & Design, Board of Communication, © Chris Christenson, for Board of Communication; (bottom) Army Chaplain, © British Forces Germany.

* * *

First published in 1996 by SAINT ANDREW PRESS
121 George Street, Edinburgh EH2 4YN
on behalf of the BOARD of COMMUNICATION of the CHURCH of SCOTLAND

British Library Cataloguing in Publication Data
A catalogue record for
this book is available
from the British Library

ISBN 0861532260

Printed by BPC Magazines Ltd.